Mighty Machines
FIRE TRUCKS
AND RESCUE VEHICLES

Jean Coppendale

QED Publishing

Copyright © QED Publishing 2007

First published in the UK in 2007 by
QED Publishing
A Quarto Group company
226 City Road
London EC1V 2TT

www.qed-publishing.co.uk

A Catalogue record for this book is available from the British Library.

ISBN 978 1 84538 893 5

Written by Jean Coppendale
Designed by Rahul Dhiman (Q2A Media)
Editor Katie Bainbridge
Picture Researcher Jyoti Sachdev (Q2A Media)
Publisher Steve Evans
Creative Director Zeta Davies
Senior Editor Hannah Ray

Printed and bound in China

Picture credits

Key: t = top, b = bottom, c = centre,
l = left, r = right, FC = front cover
Keith Levit/ **Shutterstock:** 4-5; **Photo Researchers, Inc./ Photolibrary:** 5t;
Mauritius Die Bildagentur Gmbh/ **Photolibrary:** 6-7; Micah May/ **Shutterstock:** 7t;
BIOS Gunther Michel/ **Still Pictures:** 8-9; Markus Dlouhy/ **Still Pictures:** 9b;
Oshkosh Truck Corporation: 10-11; **Index Stock Imagery/ Photolibrary:** 12-13;
Photo Researchers, Inc./ Photolibrary: 13t; Mark William Penny/ **Shutterstock:** 14-15;
LA(Phot) Emma Somerfield/ Royal Navy: 15t; **Oshkosh Truck Corporation:** 16-17;
OEAMTC: 17t; **Ford Motor Company:** 18-19; Jochen Tack/ **Still Pictures:** 19t;
REUTERS/ Fabrizio Bensch: 20b; **REUTERS**/ Guido Benschop: 20-21

Words in **bold** can be found
in the glossary on page 23.

Contents

Quick! Emergency!

If there is an accident or if someone is in trouble, an emergency **vehicle** and specially trained people rush to the scene to help.

Whenever there is a traffic accident or emergency, the police come to help out.

Fire engines, ambulances, police cars, lifeboats and rescue helicopters are all emergency vehicles. Most emergency cars and trucks have a **siren** and flashing lights so people know they are coming and can make way for them when they are racing through traffic.

Help! Fire!

Fire engines arrive quickly to put out a fire. They have tanks of water with hoses that are used to pour water onto the fire. Fire engines also have long ladders that are used to rescue people from high buildings. Firefighters wear special uniforms and helmets to protect them from the smoke and the heat of the flames.

Fire engines have metal arms at the side. This is to stop them from tipping over when their ladders are being used.

Fire engine ladders can be turned in all directions to reach people trapped in fires.

Forest fires

In some countries, forest fires can start during the summer when the weather is very hot and dry. Special aeroplanes and helicopters are used to put out these fires.

A tank full of water is carried underneath the aeroplane or helicopter. **Pilots** can open the water tank using special controls.

As this Firehawk helicopter flies over the forest it drops tons of water onto the fire below.

Helicopters are also used to rescue people, or animals, from hard-to-reach places. This is a mountain rescue helicopter carrying a dog to safety.

Airport accidents

Special equipment is needed to fight fires in airports. This is because aeroplanes are very big and airports and aeroplanes are usually filled with hundreds of people.

Airport fire trucks are built to put out a fire on an aeroplane and rescue any **passengers** trapped on board the plane.

This airport truck has special lights at the front to see through thick smoke.

Harbour **Firefighter**

The **harbour** in New York, in the United States, is used by hundreds of people every day. If a fire starts, the New York City Fire Department has a special boat called *Firefighter* which goes to the rescue.

The boat carries extra-long hoses and big water tanks to put out fires quickly and stop them from spreading.

Fireboats can pump lots of water into a fire and can rescue both people and **goods**.

Other harbours have fireboats, too, that put out fires on ships and rescue passengers.

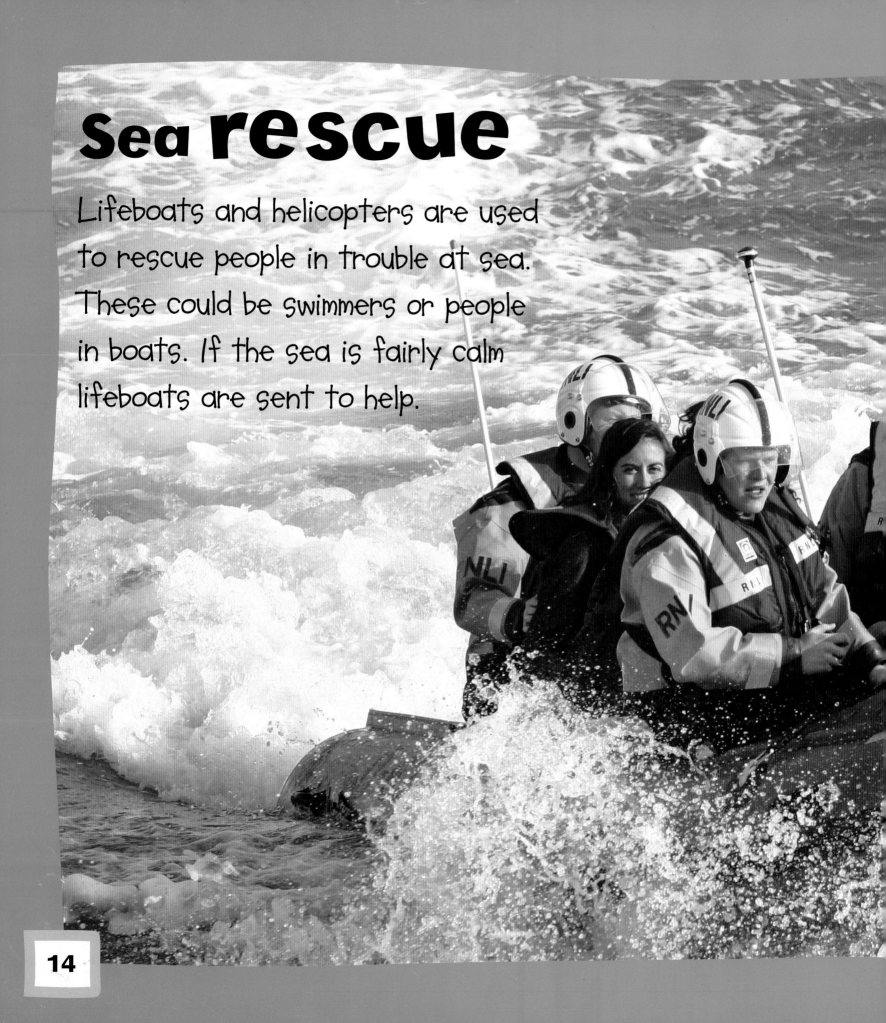

Sea rescue

Lifeboats and helicopters are used to rescue people in trouble at sea. These could be swimmers or people in boats. If the sea is fairly calm lifeboats are sent to help.

A helicopter arrives to rescue people from a sinking boat.

If the sea is very rough and it is not safe for the lifeboats, helicopters are used to **winch** people to safety.

Send an ambulance!

If someone has been badly **injured** or suddenly becomes very ill, you call an ambulance. The ambulance puts on its flashing light and loud siren and rushes to help the person, or take them to the hospital.

Inside the back of an ambulance is a bed, medical equipment and somewhere for the **paramedics** to sit.

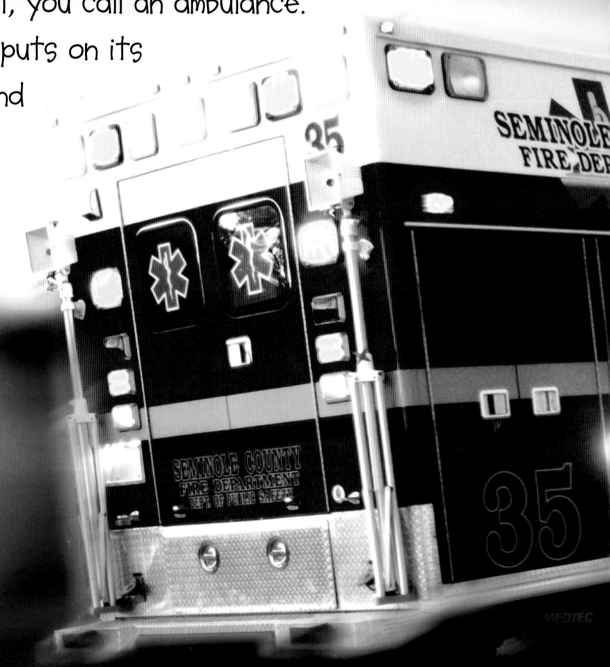

Some places are difficult to reach by road so an air ambulance helicopter is used instead.

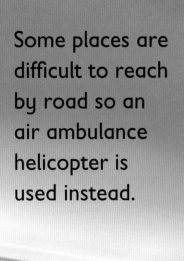

Paramedics are people trained to look after the sick or injured person inside the ambulance.

Police on their way!

Police cars are very fast and can race to the scene of a crime or accident. The police drivers have been specially trained to drive cars at high speed on busy roads and motorways.

Police cars have computers so that the officers can check information, such as if a car is stolen or not.

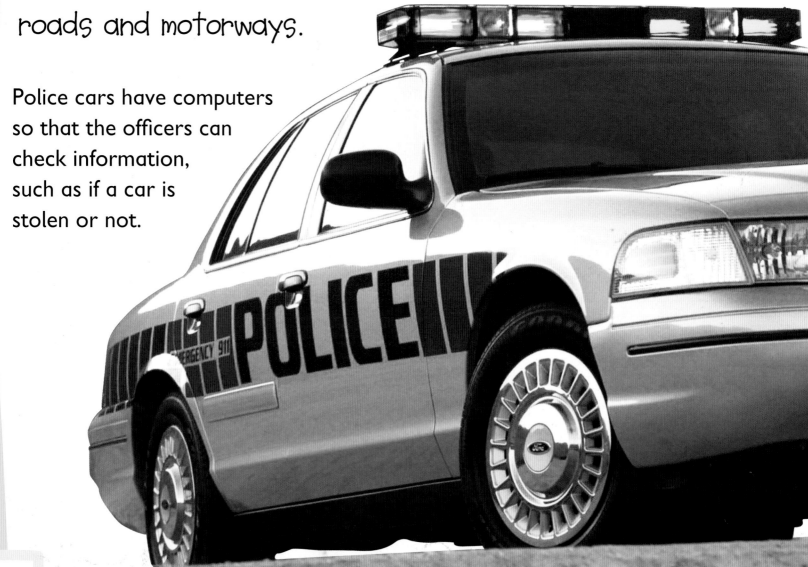

Sometimes a police helicopter is used to chase people on the roads who are speeding, or **criminals** who are trying to escape.

Motorbike patrol

In very crowded cities, some police use motorbikes to help them reach an accident quickly or chase criminals through busy streets.

Sometimes motorbike police travel with the cars of important people, to keep them safe.

Motorbike police always wear safety helmets and they have to be specially trained to ride their bikes.

Activities

- Start your own picture collection of emergency vehicles. Group them together, for example: ambulances, fire engines, police cars and so on. Which are your favourites? Why?

- Do you know what each of these emergency vehicles is used for? What can you see in each picture?

- On a big sheet of paper, draw your favourite emergency vehicle. Then imagine there is a telephone call. There has been an accident. Quick, you must help! Make up a story about what happens next.

- Which vehicle do you think a police officer would drive?

Glossary

Criminals
People who have broken the law, by doing something such as stealing.

Goods
Goods could be things such as clothes, food, cars or books. They can be moved by boat, plane, train or truck.

Harbour
A place where ships and boats can stay that is safe. This is where boats unload and collect their goods and where passenger boats pick up and drop off people.

Injured
When someone has been hurt.

Paramedics
The men and women who drive the ambulance and look after injured people until they reach the hospital.

Passengers
People who travel inside a car, bus, train, boat or aeroplane who are not driving.

Pilots
The people who fly planes.

Siren
A loud noise which is used by emergency vehicles when they are travelling very fast so that they can warn other vehicles on the road that they are coming through.

Vehicle
A car, truck or motorbike or anything else that travels on the road.

Winch
To pull someone on board a plane or helicopter using a rope.

Index